WHEN THE TREE FALLS

Jane Clarke was born in 1961 and grew up on a farm in Co. Roscommon. She lives with her partner in Glenmalure, Co. Wicklow, where she combines writing with her work as a creative writing tutor and group facilitator. She holds a BA in English and Philosophy from Trinity College, Dublin, and an MPhil in Writing from the University of South Wales, and has a background in psychoanalytic psychotherapy.

Her first collection, *The River*, was published by Bloodaxe Books in 2015. It was shortlisted for the Royal Society of Literature's Ondaatje Prize, given for a distinguished work of fiction, non-fiction or poetry evoking the spirit of a place. In 2016 she won the Hennessy Literary Award for Emerging Poetry and the inaugural Listowel Writers' Week Poem of the Year Award. She was awarded an Arts Council of Ireland Literary Bursary in 2017.

All the Way Home, Jane's illustrated booklet of poems in response to a First World War family archive held in the Mary Evans Picture Library, London, was published by Smith|Doorstop in 2019, and was followed by her second book-length collection from Bloodaxe, *When the Tree Falls*. Jane also edited *Origami Doll: New and Collected Shirley McClure* (Arlen House, 2019), and guest-edited *The North* 61: Irish Issue (The Poetry Business, 2019) with Nessa O'Mahony.

www.janeclarkepoetry.ie

JANE CLARKE

When the Tree Falls

BLOODAXE BOOKS

Copyright © Jane Clarke 2019

ISBN: 978 1 78037 480 2

First published 2019 by
Bloodaxe Books Ltd,
Eastburn,
South Park,
Hexham,
Northumberland NE46 1BS.

www.bloodaxebooks.com
For further information about Bloodaxe titles
please visit our website and join our mailing list
or write to the above address for a catalogue.

Supported using public funding by

**ARTS COUNCIL
ENGLAND**

Cover design: Neil Astley & Pamela Robertson-Pearce.

Printed in Great Britain by Bell & Bain Limited, Glasgow, Scotland, on
acid-free paper sourced from mills with FSC chain of custody certification.

For Dora and Charlie Clarke

ACKNOWLEDGEMENTS

My thanks to the editors of the following publications where several of these poems first appeared: *The Irish Times, Poetry Ireland Review, New Hibernia Review, The North, Compass, And Other Poems, The High Window, One, Prelude, Numéro Cinque, Eat Darling Eat, Washing Windows Anthology*, edited by Alan Hayes (Arlen House 2017), *The Lea-Green Down*, edited by Eileen Casey (Fiery Arrow Press, 2018) and *The Fish Anthology 2015*, edited by Clem Cairns and Julia Walton (Fish Publishing).

Thanks also to RTE Radio One's *Sunday Miscellany*, RTE Lyric FM's *Poetry File*, Near FM, UCD Library's Irish Poetry Reading Archive and the *Words Lightly Spoken* podcast where several of these poems were first broadcast.

I wish to gratefully acknowledge the Arts Council of Ireland for the award of a literary bursary in 2017 and also Culture Ireland for supporting readings in the UK and North America. I am very grateful to my editor, Neil Astley, and all at Bloodaxe Books.

Many thanks to my companions in poetry for their invaluable encouragement and suggestions, especially Eithne Hand, Jessica Traynor, Rosamund Taylor, Catherine Phil MacCarthy, Stuart Pickford and Geraldine Mitchell. Thanks also to Penelope Shuttle, Moniza Alvi, Eina McHugh, Mary Ryan and the much-missed Shirley McClure. My gratitude to my family and friends and always and ever to Isobel O'Duffy.

CONTENTS

11 Ryegrass

12 He stood at the top of the stairs

13 That I could

14 The Rod

15 Nettles

16 Cattle Stick

17 sculling

18 Sika Whistle

19 When winter comes

20 Birthing the Lamb

22 Some days

23 The Hurley-maker

24 Point of Departure

25 In Glasnevin

26 Those days

27 Polling Station

28 Metastasis

29 Copper Soles

30 you pull yourself up

31 Swim

32 willowherb

33 The Roof Rack

34 Camping at Bearna

35 Hers

36 The trouble

37 Map

38 Mammogram

39 When he falls asleep

40 Promise

41 Barometer

42 Planting Trees

43 I've got you

44   Together

45   Blue Cards

46   Cypress

47   *'At last! Are you here at last?'*

48   Night Nurse

49   Respects

50   Dunamon

51   Moon

52   Gone

53   Lullaby

54   When we left him

55   Aftergrass

56   The Finest Specimen

58   The Yellow Jumper

59   I imagine him telling me over the phone

60   When the tree falls

61   Kelly's Garden

63   NOTES

When the tree falls, how can the shadow stand?

MARY LAVIN, 'In the Middle of the Fields'

Ryegrass

his time is precious as a dry spell
when there's silage to be cut

later he'll wake breathless
and we'll be calling

for the ambulance again
but this sunlit evening

how to stop him
walking the Hill Field

where every blade of ryegrass
stands tall and tufted as May

He stood at the top of the stairs

insisting he could go down himself
but, like a frightened bullock refusing
the crush, his body wouldn't move

from the spot where I used to sit
in the dark listening to rows in the kitchen
when my mother showed him the bill

from the shop. He stood at the top
of the stairs in a fever that came on him
as fast as nightfall in winter,

steep, narrow steps between him
and the ambulance ticking
outside the back door.

He stood there in checked pyjamas
and thick Wellington socks,
in the house where he was born

and swore he would never leave.
I held him from behind,
my brother in front

coaxing with a tenderness
I'd never seen between them,
come on Dad, just one step, one step.

That I could

That I could take away from him
these long days in the hospital,

the digging for a vein in his arm,
the drip that stops him sleeping,

the pain that makes him whisper,
Jesus Christ, oh, Jesus Christ.

That I could take him back
to his cobblestones and barn,

his rooks in the birch trees, his nettles
and ditches, limestone and bog.

That I could find the words to tell him
what he will always be,

horse chestnut petals falling pink in the yard,
the well hidden in a blackthorn thicket,

a summer evening's hush,
cattle standing orange in the shallows.

The Rod

He's waiting for you,
the cardiac nurse hands me
a basin of water, washcloth, towel.

I hold the mirror steady
as he lathers, then sweeps
the razor down and across

paper-thin skin. He nicks
his upper lip, right cheek and chin,
daubs at the blood with witch hazel,

then tells me he used to bite his lip
till it bled to stop his hand shaking
when the Master raised the rod,

back when his palms
were soft as tamarisk moss.

Nettles

We thrashed ashplants
    through chest-high clumps,

daring them to sting bare knees.
    By evening our legs were dotted

with swellings like hives,
    rubbed dock leaf green.

Grandpa flattened the patch in minutes
    with the swishing sweep of his scythe,

told us nettle porridge, charlock and carrageen
    saved countless famine lives.

A weed-riven field
    was shameful as unsaved hay

but always a few stood ragtag in corners,
    where caterpillars pulled leaves into a tent

and, bound with silken thread,
    lay safe in their nettle beds.

Cattle Stick

Pull a sapling from the ditch,
ash, sally or hazel,

pliable and strong
with a solid root for ballast.

Trim it with your pocketknife
to fit your height,

whittle side-shoots and buds
till it's smooth to your hand.

Keep it close,
in a kitchen corner

or in the eave run
above the back door;

you'll come to depend on it
when you're down the fields

herding, dosing in the pen,
loading calves onto a lorry

or walking round the mart
with the other men.

sculling

all morning   they roar in the pen

      long-legged weanlings   fawn skewbald roan

a tenon saw   searing iron

               forceps and disinfectant

on the wall above

           the cattle crush and calf cradle

afterwards   my brother wields

           the yard brush

      black bristles sweeping up

               horn buds blood and muck

Sika Whistle

First it rises,
a mournful call,
like nothing will ever come right again,

then it descends –
a whistle that shreds the evening mist,
coming from high on Mullacor

where two stags stand
head to head in brindled bracken,
like father and son smouldering

in the cattle pen, taking each other's measure,
ready for battle,
their antlers sharpened on tree trunks.

When winter comes

remember what the blacksmith
knows – dim light is best

at the furnace, to see the colours
go from red to orange

to yellow, the forging heat
that tells the steel is ready

to be held in the mouth
of the tongs and it's time

to lengthen and narrow
with the ring of the hammer

on the horn of an anvil,
to bend until the forgiving metal

has found its form,
then file the burrs,

remove sharp edges,
smooth the surface,

polish with a grinding stone
and see it shine like gold.

Birthing the Lamb

Almost dawn, a March wind
whistles bitter through the shed

where the boy kneels to a ewe
panting in the corner. Waters

broken, eyes closed, lip curled,
she strains with every contraction.

His arm is far inside her
but his fingers can't find a hoof,

not even the tip of a nose
to guide him. Chest thumping,

staccato breath, he tries
to remember what his father said:

take it slow, good lad,
push back her head,

slip in your hand, reach for a leg,
that's it, cup the   hoof,

now ease it forward, don't pull
or jerk, just a steady pressure.

Streaked yellow and red,
the lamb slithers out,

gives a cough, a splutter,
shakes its head.

Taking her time,
the ewe licks off the mucus

and nuzzles her newborn
to its feet. The boy sits back

in the straw on his heels.
For a moment he forgets,

and turns to tell his father
it was the best, the best feeling.

Some days

it's like ploughing in Wexford,
not a stone to be found and the soil
dark as a night without stars.

You grease the bearings,
set the check chains, tighten nuts
and bolts, mark the headland line,

leaving space at the end to turn
the plough and realign the tractor.
The trick is in keeping

the first furrow straight. From high
in the cab, you look over your shoulder
at black-headed gulls, lapwings,

starlings, rooks in their thousands,
hurtling from all directions
to follow the plough.

The Hurley-maker

Under the green-grey bark of ash
he seeks malleable wood to shape
from curving handle to rounded *bas*.

He thins the body till it bends
like a bow, springs like a whip,
then planes and sands it

sleek as a thoroughbred's pelt.
He's seen his hurleys hoosh cows
up the lane after milking, knock

hogweed out of a ditch, hoist buckets
from a tank, lift ladybirds to count
their spots. He's watched young lads

practise roll lifts, dribbles and solos
the way ravens play with the wind.
Years he's waited for his county

to raise the cup but the day
his hurley struck two men kissing
was the first time he thought to give up.

Point of departure

A Sunday evening in January.

My father is taking me to the train
because my mother can't; her heart
is broken over what I told her.

Just my father and me,

unused to this time together,
quiet except for the engine's hum
and the sweep of wipers

but in his silence I hear a rhythm –

he's cutting thistles with a scythe,
a gate opens
into a meadow I have never seen.

In Glasnevin

(for Elizabeth O'Farrell and Julia Grenan)

Finding the words carved
on their plain, granite headstone,

faithful comrade, lifelong friend,
reminds me of my grandmother

who used to say there was none of that
in her day. I wish I could ask

the faithful Julia and Elizabeth
were they grateful for the mercy

of sharing a grave, did they choose
those words to save them from shame,

did they have someone to tell
that though the words said so much,

they didn't say enough. And, when
they nursed the rebellion's wounded,

did they question the cost
of a new (free) state?

Those days

we had to claim
    a space for love
        in the half-hidden places:

a backroom in Smyths,
    the top floor of a pub
        on a lane by the Liffey.

Looking back we could say
    it was worth it
        for the welcome

when we stepped in
    from the cold,
        for the pleasure

of removing masks
    with our shrugged off coats,
        for our bodies pulsing

to *I will survive* –
    that would be comforting
        but a lie.

Polling Station

May 25th 2018

In the queue up to the door of the schoolhouse
neighbours welcome sunshine after the wettest
of wet winters; spirits lift at the sight of fields

drying out, grass thickening, calves thriving,
unstoppable growth. There's talk of young ones
speeding home to vote, swallows back to the barn.

No one asks anyone where they'll place their X –
every family has stories, left like ploughs
and harrows among thistles behind the sheds.

Metastasis

The way couch grass takes hold of a garden,
spreads seeds, runners, white rhizomes
long before we notice, the way it grows

more tenacious when we begin to dig,
gathering different names – dog grass,
scutch grass, quick grass, twitch grass,

the way it creeps along the ground,
then sends a root deep down,
slips silent under fences, colonises beds

and gets itself entangled through agapanthus
Midnight Blue, the way that it persists,
the way that it persists.

Copper Soles

(in memory of Shirley McClure, 1962-2016)

In an old Finnish story
the hero must build a boat from oak

to bear him home through a raging storm
but he cannot complete his work

without three magic words;
the first will secure the stern,

the second will fasten the ledges,
the third will ready the forecastle.

To find the words
he must walk across points of needles,

edges of hatchets,
blades of swords,

for which he needs shoes
with copper soles.

Dear friend,
while the doctors chase pain

around your body,
where will we find such a cobbler?

you pull yourself up

for the power and pulse
> that lifts you and your board

> > so you're standing on water

for the sound of the spray
> when a clean wave breaks

> > in hailstones around you

for the time outside time
> when you catch the gust

> > and are swept the full length of the fetch

for the wind
> like a blade to your neck

> > the tug of the swell

in the moment before
> you must bail

> > you pull yourself up

Swim

In the early days of our friendship
    we'd sit in the sun at Lacken Weir,

        teasing out thoughts and feelings
            like wool we'd washed in the Nore.

We picked the fleece apart,
    loosening briars and dander,

        fluffing the locks till the fibres,
            unmatted, were ready to rove.

We swam in the river stretching before us
    from Devil's Bit Mountain to the Barrow Bridge,

        until illness seeped in,
            stealthy as groundwater after a storm.

Tonight in St Vincent's,
    your sister and I sit by your bed

        in low light from above your pillowed head.
            Your body quivers with every breath.

Do you know we're beside you,
    can you hear us speak of you, sleek as an otter,

        slipping into the river?
        The blinds are up

and the city's twinkling from here to Kippure,
    where the Liffey rises to the whimbrel's call,

        then winds its way through darkness
            into the shallows of Dublin Bay.

willowherb

while you were leaving
the wind picked up

and tossed lithe stems
purple-pink flower heads

by the breeze block wall
of the hospital car park

clouds of seed
lifting and spinning

The Roof Rack

My brother has taken to making suggestions
for the poems I should write: one

about the stoat we saw crossing the bridge
at the bottom of the Hill Field,

its brown summer coat and black-tipped tail,
or one about the cobwebbed roof rack

that's hanging in the shed. Can't you see,
he says, it was painted each time

we changed the car; there's a speck of green
from the Prefect we had in the 50s, blue

from the Anglia, traces of red from the Cortina,
a Hillman Imp that was white.

Don't you remember, he asks, the trouble
every summer after the hay; searching

for clasps and screws that went missing
over the winter? Someone was sure

to catch their fingers, then the cattle
would break out across the river

and we'd be sent down the fields
to fetch them, the sky promising rain.

Camping at Bearna

Fifty odd miles from home
in a wind-blown, Atlantic field
she has us connecting poles,

guiding them into flaps, hoops
and eyelets, hammering pegs,
tightening guy-ropes.

The groundsheet rips, the milk
turns sour, someone drops the eggs
and more often than not

we wake to the pock, pock, pock
of raindrops. She spreads
wet towels on brambles,

keeps an eye on the tides
and watches us run bare-foot
down the bye-road to the strand.

Nothing rocks her belief –
a week at the edge of the ocean
will set her children free.

Hers

My mother said she knew, just knew I was going to be a girl,
two boys before me and two boys after, fodder for a hungry farm,
but I was hers. She taught me her tricks of the trade: it'll look
like dinner is nearly ready if the table is set when he comes in,

bread and butter will fill them up, add three drops of vinegar
to water so your mirrors and windows will gleam, cool
your fingers before rubbing lard into flour for pastry, a handful
of ground almonds will keep your fruit cake moist,

darn a few socks every night and never leave the ironing
for more than a week, don't cut off rhubarb stalks with a knife,
just twist them clean from the crown, and always hold onto
the children's allowance; a woman must have something of her own.

The trouble

between mothers and daughters
       is how to forgive

the one to whom
       you owe too much

what you see when you look
       in the mirror

how you forget you were in her
       and she is in you

or the way
       she loves you

and cannot, will not
       leave you alone

Map

She pinned a Simplicity pattern
on sky blue denim,

fed the fabric
through the machine,

sewing swirl to swirl for the skirt
that would take me away from her.

Among spools of thread,
ribbons, bias binding and zips,

she found the pinking shears
and cut the fringed hem.

A paper pattern's like a map,
she said, arrow heads give direction,

dots mark collars and pockets,
where to tuck or pleat,

notches show fittings
for waist, hips and breasts...

that was when we believed
if I followed the map

I could be
whoever I wanted to be.

Mammogram

A bed under the window, charts
on the desk and a poem on the wall

about fathers and horses and love.
While we wait for the doctor

I could talk to my mother
about the stone growing in her breast

but instead I read the poem aloud
and she tells me stories she's told before

about her father and horses
ploughing up pastureland during the war,

how they sowed, reaped and winnowed
cartloads of barley and oats.

She asks me to read it again
as when she taught me to recite

The Owl and the Pussy-cat went to sea
In a beautiful pea-green boat –

the colour of this room
where there's little

but a poem about fathers
and horses and love.

When he falls asleep

at the kitchen table and drops
another cup, my mother bends
without a word, sweeps up

the broken pieces in her hands,
looking out for shards in case
he wanders barefoot in the night.

Promise

After the talk with the palliative nurse
over cups of tea in the kitchen,
my mother says she's already asked him

to promise he'll make it through the winter –
it'll be sixty years in April, sixty years
since she walked down the aisle in her dress

of pristine lace, beaded bodice
with tiny satin-covered buttons at the nape,
a full skirt of tulle falling from her waist

to red and black tiles. Ballymoe Church
is tumbling now, stone by stone,
beneath the weight of brambles, ivy, ash.

I was eager and silly as a suck calf, she laughs,
as she readies his tablets, a whiff of silage
rising from the coats drying by the stove.

Barometer

Notebook on the kitchen table,
rota underlined in red, updates
about tablets, temperature, pain.

We pulled together like we used to
when he'd stand in the front hall
and tap-tap the glass.

When the needle rose, we mowed
the meadow where the corncrake
nested among foxtail, fescue, bent.

We raked the windrows, readied flasks
and buttered bread, mended tedder tines,
forked heaviest grass from the headland,

watching the sky, praying
for the weather to hold.

Planting Trees

Dad taught us that paper
comes from trees and the word for book

comes from beech. He showed us
the olive-grey bark, smooth as river rocks,

how to tell the light hues of young wood
from the gloom of the old

and how to count the rings – starting
at the centre, working out towards the edge.

He's unable to move from his bed,
but when we ask about the row of beech

beside the bridge, he's clear as a bell,
my father's father's father planted them,

a shelter-belt for a nursery, when the British
were giving grants for planting trees.

Tomorrow, I'll get dressed,
we'll go down to see them again.

I've got you

Through days of morphine
and titbits to tempt his appetite,
there's nowhere else to be.

I hold his teacup to his lips,
wash his face and the hands
I rarely touched.

During the night old hurts
and worries surface
like stones in a well-tilled field.

What time is it now? he asks
on the hour. He sings to himself
and murmurs lines he learned

as a child, 'All we, like sheep
have gone astray, we have turned
everyone to his own way.'

When he asks to get up
I hold his wrists,
brace my weight against his.

For a moment he's confused –
it's okay Janey, I've got you,
go on now, you can stand.

Together

I've never seen them
holding hands before

yet this seems familiar,
as if they sat every morning

in easy silence, broken
from time to time.

How are you feeling, Charlie?
Never better, dear.

Blue Cards

Winter mornings he was gone before dawn
to fairs in Ballyhaunis, Claremorris, Ballinrobe.
He came home with muck on his coat,
smelling of Shorthorns and Herefords.

Sometimes he told us who he'd met,
the blind man who knew each of his cows
by their lowing, the widow who bargained
harder than any dealer. But mostly he sat

distracted by prices, cigarette smoke
spiralling to the kitchen ceiling, blue cards
spread around the table. Today, when everyone
else was away, I wrapped him warm,

pushed his wheelchair through the haggard,
up the yard to the sheds. The cattle lifted
doleful eyes from heaps of silage.
Hello lads, he said.

Cypress

Falling in and out
of sleep all night

he suddenly struggles
to sit up.

Will you open the curtains
so we'll see the dawn when it comes?

He gazes out
at the cypress

that in his lifetime
grew higher than the house.

A tree that survived
every winter's wind,

its trunk ridged
as a raised bed ready for seed,

feathered foliage
set to sprout flower balls,

exposed roots,
worn bare as bones,

branches touching the ground,
forming a haven –

a tree to sit in,
quiet, waiting.

'At last! Are you here at last?'
(SEAMUS HEANEY, *Aeneid Book VI*)

Half-asleep on a mattress beside his bed,
I hear his question in the ember light
of the wood-burning stove.

Do you believe in heaven, a ghrá?

We've argued God and religion
since I was thirteen. Belief was a wall
between us until the day he said

without it he wouldn't know how to go on.
The wall became a hazel hedge,
sheltering finches, spiders, bees.

Do you believe in heaven, Dad?

He answers as if he's been thinking about it
all night. *All I know is I'm going somewhere
I'll meet the people I love.*

Night Nurse

If he were conscious he'd urge her
to sit beside him for questions
about her people over cups of tea

but she says no more than needs
to be said as I help her turn him, check
for bed sores, connect the morphine pump.

She tells me it won't be long, knows when
to gather the others. It happens quickly
in the end. She leaves us together

and when we're ready, helps wash
his body. My brother flings the windows open;
still dark, the air whetted with frost.

Herefords lowing from the slatted sheds,
the choir he'd have chosen. She collects
her watch, torch and glasses.

I don't want her to go. When she leaves
for home across the Curlews,
she'll be taking him with her.

Respects

From Kiltoom, Creemully, Loughglynn,
Kilbegnet, Lecarrow, Athleague,
Creggs, Carrowkeel, Ballinleg,
they come to pay their respects.

They shake hands with us, stand
by his body and bow their heads:
cattle men, sheep men, carpenters,
teachers, foresters, nurses, vets.

They say prayers, lay their hands
on his chest and bless themselves,
then fill the kitchen with the man
they knew, *a grand man altogether,*

always out early, hardy as a wild duck,
a good judge of a bullock, fierce man
to work, he had woeful hands,
a man of his word.

I slip out for a while to see
an orange globe over the Common
and a flock of whooper swans
feasting on the last of the winter grass.

Dunamon

They dig slower as they go deeper,
taking turns to heave shovels of clay,

throwing bigger stones and rocks
up into the tractor box.

Son, grandson, nephew, neighbours,
they've already gone down five feet,

when they lay their tools aside,
drink tea, light up for a smoke

and agree they couldn't have
a better day for digging a grave –

not a cloud to be seen,
sunshine melting last night's frost,

and, from the woods behind them,
a chaffinch singing his heart out.

Moon

Not that those months
        minding him were easy,

anxiety spreading like cleavers
        through a perennial bed,

sleeplessness leaving us vexed
        as wasps facing winter,

our questions circling
        ever closer to the edge,

but compared to this,
        they were white

and pink-splashed blossoms
        on briar roses in June,

dusty hedgerows mottled
        with Peacocks and Common Blues,

unmapped, grass-lined bye-roads,
        moonlight everywhere.

Gone

no dawn
in the day of gone

no spring
in the year of gone

no gate
in the wall of gone

only a gap
where he'd stand

watching the cattle
content in long grass

Lullaby

Try as he might, he couldn't hush
the baby's crying. He carried her
out to the yard, showed her pullets

pecking at scraps, ewes snuffling
oats, calves tucked up in straw
but she wouldn't be consoled.

He sat with her on a sack of barley
in the barn, lifted a handful
that smelled of molasses

and began to speak of reaping,
threshing, winnowing grain;
dust and chaff clinging to sweat

as they bent to stook sheaves.
He hummed the thrasher's
thrumming and by the time

he got to the twisters that sent
wisps of straw circling like spirits
above their heads, she slept.

When we left him

in the green plaid shirt and red tie he'd kept
for a special occasion, his good tweed jacket,
corduroy trousers and brown shoes polished

to a Sunday shine, it helped to know
he loved the earth he was buried under.
He'd wire-brush moss from the headstones,

weed the gravel, paint the high black gates.
Months later the graveyard's empty
as the stable, haggard and hayshed.

His dog's still looking for something he's lost.
Beneath our feet autumn is sprouting a feast,
not only the pink-gilled white caps

he'd bring into the kitchen on thrawneens
but egg-yellow chanterelles, pestle puffballs,
purple wood blewits, tawny grisettes.

Aftergrass

Lofts full before the end of June,
stoat kits playing in the aftergrass,

cattle clustered in dusty circles
among thickets of hazel and ash,

little egrets sentinel-still
in shallows more shallow

than we've ever seen.
I sit by my father

and tell him the sun has scorched
every blade of grass.

His headstone's not up
but the wording's agreed.

The Finest Specimen

When I was a child my father wrote the twelve days
of Roscommon fair on the back of a Players pack
and taught me to recite them as farmers used to.

He showed me where the blacksmith had inscribed
1865 on a gate – *the year Yeats was born*, he'd say.
There's one date you have to remember, your great

great great grandfather, the one with the whiskers,
was born the year of the rebellion in 1798,
any family history before that is just imagination.

He showed me a Bible with miniature print
on gossamer paper which he touched as if it were
pure gold. *This was your great-grandmother's,*

published the month of the Act of Union. He told me
old stories as if he'd lived through them.
When the turlough froze in 1816,

three neighbours walked the ice with sacks of oats
on a short-cut home from the mill; one fell into a gap,
the other two drowned trying to save him. Other stories

he seldom told, how as a boarder in Blackhall Place
he slept with his feet pointing west or how he
and my mother returned early from honeymoon

because he was lonely for the fields. Yesterday
he took out old letters, bound together with knotted string:
my brother's first letter home, another from a neighbour

thanking my grandfather for a loan, and the letter
from his grandmother to her sister on the morning
of his birth, the second last day of March, 1929.

He came unexpectedly, the finest specimen yet,
with Dad's nose and Georgie's chin,
good looking and the most formed little thing.

The Yellow Jumper

They weren't married long when she saw it,
a turtle-necked jumper in Murray's window –
yellow as happiness, as the flash on a goldfinch's wings.

She imagined him wearing it at the fairs,
standing out from all the rest in their greens
and greys. Eighteen shillings and sixpence,

she paid for it on tick, thruppence a week.
For all that he smiled on his birthday,
it remained on the back of the bedroom chair.

One day she folded and packed it in the chest
with the spare candles, letters, photographs
and the other questions she didn't ask.

She likes to think of him there, among pens
of breeding heifers, weanlings and hoggets,
splendid in yellow.

I imagine him telling me over the phone

you know the beech tree
near where the flax was retted

the one that stretched its branches
out over the river… it fell last night

One more season
and he'd have seen

the latticed roots
ripped out of the ground,

a map of the underworld
in its stone-studded mound.

I'd have asked him why
it fell – old age, wounded

heartwood, windthrow, or
root rot from too much rain?

When the tree falls

into the river
        it slows the current

                water pools
        in the hollows it makes

pike and trout
        find a new place to hide

                beetles mayfly and mites
        feed on leaf litter

the mossy trunk
        lies still as a bridge

                a kingfisher settles
        watches for minnow

branches reach for the light
        noble with new buds

Kelly's Garden

You can find him in the names of the fields:
      Kelly's Garden, Back O'Naughtons, Moll Brannan's,
          the Sand Hole, the Quarry, the Rocks.

He's stacking square bales,
      chanting *knots in and down*
          so rain won't lodge in their hearts.

March and he's cursing
      merciless wind –
          cattle running amuck.

He's laughing at McAleer's joke
      about the father who welcomes
          his eldest home

from Alberta or Azerbaijan
      with the only question that matters –
          Were there many on the bus?

You can hear him in the jackdaws'
      tchack, tchack,
          up high on galvanised roofs,

and in his whistling
      that rises and falls like the curlew
          calling from Emla bog.

NOTES

'In Glasnevin' won the inaugural Listowel Writers' Week Poem of the Year Award at the Irish Book Awards 2016. The poem is dedicated to the lifelong companions, Elizabeth O'Farrell and Julia Grenan, who were nurses and couriers in the Easter Rising 1916 and are buried together in the republican plot at Glasnevin Cemetery, Dublin.

'Swim' was written in response to a painting by Carol Wood, for a Roscommon County Council exhibition, *A Poem, An Image*, and is featured in a film by Bailey & Blake for their series, *The River Liffey Stories*.

'Mammogram': the poem referred to is 'Lone Patrol' by Mary Noonan, which is on display as part of the Galway University Hospitals Arts Trust *Poems for Patience* initiative.

'Blue Cards': a blue card is a bovine animal passport.

'When we left him': a thrawneen is a stalk or stem of grass.